DIRECTIONS 1

READING SKILLS

John Cooper

Oliver & Boyd

For the pupil

For years you have been *learning to read*. Gradually you have been recognising more and more words and understanding more difficult pages of print. These are all very important reading skills.

As you are now *reading to learn* by yourself, it is important for you to practise and develop other skills which will enable you to read more efficiently.

Think of why you are reading. It may be for information, to decide on a course of action, for enjoyment or some other purpose.

How do you read? There are different ways of reading. You probably read street names, numbers on buses or signs outside shops very quickly. This skill of very rapid reading may be used a lot, but you will need other skills when you read instructions, school books and work-cards which must be studied carefully and given much thought.

As you work your way through this book you are going to develop and practise skills you need to make you a better and more efficient reader.

Skills are introduced one at a time and you are given practice so that you can improve and feel confident in one skill before moving on to the next.

For the teacher

The teachers' task in the middle years is of a two-fold nature. First, they should ensure consolidation and development of basic skills already acquired — identification of words, pronunciation, acquisition of word meanings, and facility in tackling words, sentences and paragraphs — and, secondly, they should concern themselves with the more advanced skills required by the pupil in proceeding more rapidly and delving more deeply into the world of literature.

It seems to be commonly assumed that pupils will acquire these skills fortuitously, just by reading. Many adults argue that any achievement that they have made in this direction is entirely independent of any training received in the primary or, indeed, the secondary school.

The purpose in presenting the following material is to enable pupils *to study* and *to practise* the more advanced skills they require for independent reading. Teachers will discover the kind of help each pupil needs and can group pupils for practice sessions. While practice periods for reading improvement ensure direct attention to learning, practice will not be an end in itself but should give the pupil greater confidence and help to improve his reading in general.

Contents

1. What's it all about?
Reading for main ideas

SORTING OUT

When we read, we should try to find out the main thought in the writer's mind. Before considering longer passages let us look at a few lists of words.

If I write *Great Britain, Malawi, Egypt, China, Russia,* what am I thinking about? For an answer or title we might write *Countries.*

In the same way look at each of the following lists of words and suggest a title for each.

1. (a) Blackbirds, canaries, sparrows, budgerigars, gulls.
   (b) Daffodils, daisies, roses, sweet peas, carnations.
   (c) Aeroplanes, trains, ferries, buses, liners.
   (d) Boots, slippers, shoes, sandals, wellingtons.

2. (a) Cottages, bungalows, flats, villas.
   (b) Flies, bluebottles, beetles, wasps, bees.
   (c) Pianos, accordions, organs, guitars, violins.
   (d) Football, cricket, rounders, tennis, badminton.
   (e) Oak, ash, elm, chestnut, beech, willow.

3. (a) Tables, chairs, sideboards, wardrobes, beds.
   (b) Cups, saucers, plates, bowls, jugs.
   (c) Wood, coke, coal, gas, oil.
   (d) Novels, dictionaries, encyclopaedias, manuals, atlases, biographies.
   (e) Trousers, coats, vests, jerseys, socks.

Let us consider another list.

	Title
France, Germany, Holland, Denmark, Belgium	Countries

The suggested title is *Countries*. Perhaps you could think of a more exact title. Great Britain is omitted so you might suggest *Foreign Countries*. This would be correct and more exact. You might notice that each country is in Europe and suggest *European Countries*. Again, this would be correct and more exact than *Countries*.

Now look at each of the following lists and suggest a more exact title for each group.

	Title
4. (a) Cows, pigs, horses, sheep, goats.	Animals
(b) Lions, tigers, elephants, kangaroos, zebras.	Animals
(c) Buses, cars, lorries, vans, coaches, bicycles.	Transport
(d) Yachts, hovercraft, liners, ferries, canoes.	Transport
(e) Apple trees, peach trees, plum trees, pear trees, cherry trees.	Trees
5. (a) Daffodils, tulips, hyacinths, snowdrops, crocuses.	Flowers
(b) Buttercups, daisies, dandelions, bluebells, thistles.	Flowers
(c) Football, netball, rugby, basket-ball, volley-ball.	Games
(d) Mutton, pork, beef, venison, veal, ham.	Food
(e) Cabbages, lettuces, potatoes, turnips, cauliflowers.	Food
6. (a) Strawberries, raspberries, gooseberries, blackcurrants, cherries.	Food
(b) Caps, hats, turbans, berets, hoods, sou'westers.	Clothes
(c) Cola, limeade, orangeade, lemonade, ginger beer.	Liquids
(d) Spade, hoe, rake, fork, trowel.	Tools
(e) Salmon, herring, cod, haddock, trout.	Food

5

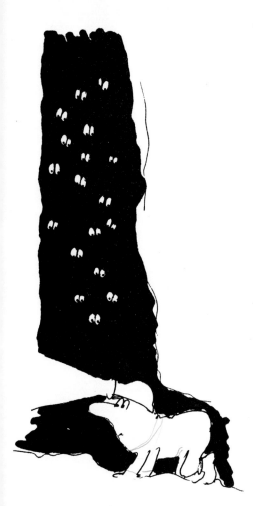

TITLES

After you have read the following paragraph carefully, study the titles underneath it.

Over the past few years bats have been declining in numbers. The high price of bat skins encourages the hunters who are out to make money. Also, as potholing becomes more popular as a sport, bats are more likely to be disturbed during their long winter sleep in caves and tunnels. If bats are disturbed too often they will die. It is little wonder that we hear reports that some species are already low in number.

    (a) The long sleep of the bat;
    (b) Potholing as a sport;
    (c) The decrease in the number of bats.

Which of the three titles best expresses the main thought of the paragraph?

The writer mentions "the long sleep of the bat", but that is not the main thought in his mind. He also mentions "potholing as a sport" since it accounts for possible disturbance.
The main thought in the writer's mind is
    (c) The decrease in the number of bats.
The other things are mentioned to explain why this is happening.

Read the following paragraph. Below it are three titles. Write out the one which best describes what the paragraph is about.

George always looked forward to Saturdays. How delightful to think there was no need to get up early, no last-minute rush and no school. If the sun shone he would play football in the park; if it rained he would watch television. It was true that he enjoyed the youth club on Tuesday evenings and the inter-school games on Wednesdays, but then he also had to go to school on those days. Saturday could be a day of relaxation or excitement or both, and, best of all, a chance to stay up late at night.

    (a) George the footballer;
    (b) Best day of the week;
    (c) Saturday television.

MAIN IDEAS

Read the following paragraphs. After each there are suggestions as to what is the main thought in the writer's mind. Decide which is the correct one in each case.

Sound is made by something moving back and forth. If you stretch a rubber band and pluck it, you can watch it vibrating and listen to the sound it makes. A mosquito's wings hum and leaves rustle in the wind. These are different kinds of sounds, but when the mosquito's wings are at rest and the wind dies away the sounds stop. To have sound there must be movement.

This paragraph is about
   (a) sounds made by mosquito's wings;
   (b) movement making sounds;
   (c) stretching elastic bands.

James had read that other animals are frightened of the lion's roar. Perhaps that was true but he gave it little thought until the night when he watched a circus on television. As the lions left the ring, Leo roared loudly. Suddenly, Monty, James's cat, scampered out of sight beneath the settee and Tim, his spaniel who had been asleep on the mat, barked furiously and raced to the door. The two pet animals were certainly very frightened.

This paragraph is about
   (a) The circus show on television;
   (b) The lion's frightening roar;
   (c) Tim, the spaniel.

For most children the month before Christmas cannot pass quickly enough. There will be holidays from school, the shops will look bright and gay and perhaps there will be snow on the ground. Which girl or boy does not dream of the presents to be opened on Christmas morning? Later there is Christmas dinner, and in the evening party games, television or just a rest from the excitement of the day. But it all seems so slow in coming – a whole month away.

This passage is about
  (a) holidays from school;
  (b) looking forward to Christmas;
  (c) playing party games;
  (d) presents.

Let us all help to keep our streets tidy. It is so sad to see some people dropping litter anywhere they please. Not only that, but they are often the ones who complain that street cleaners do not keep our streets clean. If only everyone would put their litter into the bins provided or, better still, take it home, our streets would look attractive, the police could spend more time catching criminals instead of litter louts and the street cleaners would have less unnecessary work to do. But everyone must help, and that includes you.

This passage is mainly about
  (a) the work of the police;
  (b) the work of street cleaners;
  (c) the prevention of litter;
  (d) the arrest of criminals.

SUMMARIES

Can you find the main ideas in a longer passage? Read the following three paragraphs and from the list below each one select what you think is the main idea in that paragraph. (Write the whole answer each time.)

There was excitement in the air as the people of Paris crowded the banks of the Seine in their thousands to see if Fulton's ship could really sail against the current of the river. Some thought it possible, but many more doubted it. Fulton himself was very worried about the possibility of failure. He watched anxiously as smoke poured from the funnel. The paddle had almost completed its first turn and the ship lay still. Would it be able to move the ship forward? As the paddle gathered speed the ship slowly but surely began to move up river. Fulton sighed with relief. He turned and smiled to the cheering crowds for he knew, and they knew, that he had proved his critics wrong.

This paragraph is about
 (a) the size of the crowds on the river bank;
 (b) the success of Fulton's ship in France;
 (c) what Fulton's critics said.

Although Fulton was very distressed to find that so few people in England were interested in what he thought was a very exciting invention, he set sail for America determined to build a new steamship there. He made plans, bought the necessary materials and employed American workers. There were many difficulties and much hard work and delay but he pressed on with great enthusiasm, and by the summer of 1807 was proud to have succeeded in his work in America. The steamship *Clermont* was ready for sea trials.

This paragraph is mainly about
 (a) Fulton's disappointment in England;
 (b) building the new ship Clermont *in America;*
 (c) the slow progress of Fulton's work.

9

Fulton planned that his new ship, the *Clermont*, should prove herself in trials by sailing from New York to Albany. The distance is 278 kilometres and it was indeed a very long voyage for a new steamship of such a type to sail. Although Fulton was very confident many doubted whether the *Clermont* could complete it as they watched her starting to steam upstream. But thirty-two hours later she reached Albany. This was even better than Fulton had expected, and now he knew that experts would, at last, take note since the trials had been so successful.

This paragraph is mainly about
    (a) the distance from New York to Albany;
    (b) what the experts would think;
    (c) the successful trials of the Clermont.

Now look at your three answers for the paragraphs on this page and page 9.

Would you agree that they give you a very brief summary of the story?

This is the famous steamship, Comet, *which first sailed on the River Clyde four years after the* Clermont's *historic journey.*

On page 12 there are five paragraphs.
Here are five titles, one for each paragraph.
See if you can choose the correct title for each paragraph.

(a) *Bees and wasps sting when annoyed.*
(b) *Tropical insects are more of a problem than British insects.*
(c) *Bees sting once, wasps many times.*
(d) *Mosquitos may spread disease as they bite.*
(e) *Biting insects often carry disease.*

You can set your answers out like this.

Paragraph   *Title*
                             (Write only the letter each time)
    (1)   (e)
    (2)
    (3)
    (4)
    (5)

11

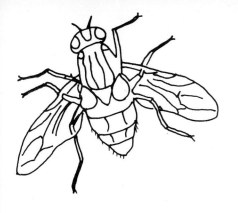

Read all five paragraphs before you choose a title for any of them.

1. You will be able to recognise many different kinds of insects. Some of them you may like, but others may frighten you because they are liable to bite. Sometimes this can be serious because a biting insect may carry disease. If it happens to bite and suck the blood of a person suffering from some disease and then later on bites a healthy person, it injects some of the disease germs into his blood and so infects him with the disease. In this way diseases spread rapidly in some parts of the world.

2. The mosquito is a biting insect. With its sharp beak, rather like a tiny hollow needle, it pierces your skin. It does not mean to harm you but to feed on your blood. In order to suck blood up through its minute tube, it injects some of its saliva to keep your blood from clotting in the tube. It is this saliva which causes the itch in your skin, but much more serious is the fact that it may contain disease germs with which you may be infected.

3. Not all irritating insects actually bite us. Some of them sting. The bee and the wasp carry a sting at the tip of the tail. This has nothing to do with feeding but is used in attack, usually on a person who has been annoying them. Their sting is also like a hollow tube but it does not suck up blood. It pierces the skin and injects a poison which causes pain and discomfort. We would be well advised not to annoy bees and wasps.

4. There is one marked difference between wasps and bees. The sting of the wasp is sharp and smooth and, therefore, it can sting many times without harm to itself. But the sting of the bee is barbed and extremely difficult to pull out of the skin. Very often it is left behind. When the sting has been torn out, the bee suffers such severe injury that it dies. Normally, therefore, a bee can sting only once.

5. Insects are a very serious problem in tropical regions of the world. Large sums of money are spent there to destroy insects before they spread disease. We are fortunate in this country because few insects carry disease, even though they may often cause us a great deal of discomfort.

Now try the following

1. If you had enough money would you go on a cruise in the Caribbean? Perhaps one day you will be one of the lucky ones.

2. As you sail among the islands your guide may suggest the boat should anchor near the shore. When he tells you to look down into the clear water at the coral below, you may gaze in wonder at a magnificently coloured fish. You will be looking at no ordinary fish but at the tropical flying fish. Suddenly it may burst through the surface and skim over the sea displaying its colourful wings.

3. Perhaps it is full of glee or it may, just in time, have seen the open fierce jaws of the barracuda. When full grown the barracuda is nearly two metres long. It lurks quietly around on the sea bed, and looks harmless until it shows its vicious teeth, a sight which frightens the flying fish and causes it to flee.

4. Perhaps a few fishermen are standing, armed with spears, in a small boat nearby. Their patience seems endless but they are looking intently not at the flying fish but for a glimpse of the barracuda. It is popular with the islanders, indeed it is one of their favourite dishes. If it stays still on the sea bed, spears will dart through the water. When one has been caught the fishermen move on a short distance to look for another.

Which of the following is the main idea in the writer's mind?

Paragraph 2	The beautiful flying fish
	The boat at anchor
	The clear tropical sea

Paragraph 3	The sea bed
	The barracuda
	The teeth

Paragraph 4	The fishermen are armed
	The fishermen are eager to catch the barracuda
	The fishermen are patient

Speech

Teacher:	Now we shall read. Start where we left off yesterday.
Pupil (reading):	Thee leetle sheep –
Teacher:	Not "thee", say "the".
Pupil:	The leetle sheep –
Teacher:	No! The little ship!
Pupil:	The little sheep –
Teacher:	Not sheep, you ass, but ship.
Pupil:	The leetle ship –
Teacher:	Damn it! Are you deaf? I've already said "little ship", not "leetle ship". Start all over again.
Pupil:	Thee little ship –

and so on.

(*Colditz* – P. R. Reid)

The teacher is teaching
  (a) how to spell
  (b) how to pronounce
  (c) how to understand meaning.

Prosecutor:	I suggest, Mr. Jones, that you did see Tom Davies at the road junction.
Mr. Jones:	I was not looking in the direction of the road junction. I don't know if he, Tom Davies, was there.
Prosecutor:	In which direction were you looking?
Mr. Jones:	I can't remember.
Prosecutor:	So how do you remember you were not looking towards the junction when Tom Davies passed?
Mr. Jones:	Because if Tom Davies was at the junction, as you say, I would have seen him.
Prosecutor:	How do you know you would have seen him?
Mr. Jones:	Because you say he was there, and I know him, and if I had looked towards the junction, I would have seen him.
Prosecutor:	You are lying. You did see Tom Davies at the road junction.

The main question is whether
  (a) Tom Davies was at the junction,
  (b) Mr. Jones was looking towards the junction, or
  (c) Mr. Jones saw Tom Davies at the junction.

Give a title

Can you suggest a suitable title for the following passage?

Things went pretty well for the rest of that day. It continued to rain and Sue decided on a kitchen party.

The games were mostly guessing rice and barley and sago blindfold by the feel of them, and drinking eggcups full of water with salt or sugar or vinegar in and saying what each was.

There was also tossing in a blanket – but this did not amount to much as Sue and Bob could not manage a real toss and merely jiggled the occupants about or tipped them out on the floor. And there was making the round of the kitchen without touching the floor. Chairs, the table, the window-ledge, an open cupboard (if you could get round the door), the fender and such things provided footholds. Sometimes the stretch from one spot to another was enormous and though Bob might manage it, the twins had to risk a spring. The whole party was a great success and the younger children quite forgot that Mother and Daddy had gone away.

(*The Children who lived in a Barn* – Eleanor Graham)

October, 1st.

Dear Daddy-Long-Legs,

I love College and I love you for sending me – I'm very, very happy, and so excited every moment of the time that I can scarcely sleep. You can't imagine how different it is from the John Grier Home. I never dreamed there was such a place in the world. I'm feeling sorry for everybody who isn't a girl and who can't come here; I am sure the College you attended when you were a boy couldn't have been so nice.

(*Daddy-Long-Legs* – Jean Webster)

The main thought in the writer's mind is?

Suggest a title for each paragraph

1. In the spring of 1746 Bonnie Prince Charlie faced many great difficulties. The morale of his army was low after the wearisome retreat from Derby and the frequent disagreements amongst the clansmen. The long cold winter made many long to go home and forget about war. Worst of all, the soldiers were short of food and the Prince had no money with which to pay them or buy supplies.

2. He looked to France for assistance. King Louis expressed sympathy and friendship but these were of no immediate help. He did not send troops who could have aided the cause and been a match for Bonnie Prince Charlie's enemies. But help was sent in the form of a large sum of money, perhaps £20 000, and for this Charles was very grateful.

3. The journey of the sloop, *Le Prince Charles*, which carried the gold, was no pleasure trip. Captain Talbot and his crew were in a state of fear and alarm all the way from France lest an English ship should appear. A sloop would be no match for a man-of-war. All went well until they approached the Moray Firth. Captain Talbot beat a hasty retreat when he spotted British warships on guard. But it was too late. The *Sheerness* gave chase northwards, through the Pentland Firth.

4. Realising he could not outrun the *Sheerness*, Captain Talbot tried a more cunning plan. With the approach of evening he steered into the Kyle of Tongue hoping that the warship would not follow. The *Sheerness* kept coming so *Le Prince Charles* was deliberately run ashore to ensure that the warship could not come alongside to take the gold since it could sail only in deeper waters.

5. As darkness fell the crew decided they must speedily abandon ship and get ashore. *Le Prince Charles* might well have been damaged as she grounded. This would have been nothing compared to the destruction that the guns of the *Sheerness* began to inflict on her from long range. The sounds of gun-fire might well attract Charlie's enemies from the surrounding areas. Not only had each man to get ashore but he had to take a quantity of gold with him.

6. Their luck on landing was remarkable. They approached the house of William Mackay of Melness to discover he was a strong supporter of their side and he welcomed them. In his house, enjoying the warmth of the fire and the refreshing food he provided, they rested thankful for their escape from the death that had seemed so near. In the early hours of the morning William Mackay sold them two horses to carry their money and sent his son to guide them to their Prince near Inverness.

7. But their high spirits did not last long. An enemy supporter, Lord Reay, who lived on the other side of the Kyle, sent armed men to delay their progress. While his snipers held up the Jacobites, word was sent for other government supporters to come and capture the men and the gold. Very soon all avenues of escape were blocked. In despair Captain Talbot and his men broke open the boxes and threw the gold pieces into Loch Hakon or in the heather and then surrendered.

8. What of the gold? Is it still lying there in the silt at the bottom of the loch?

2. Tell me more
Reading for details

CLASSIFYING

On many occasions all you will wish to know are the main thoughts or ideas in what you are reading. This may be the case when you are reading a story.

But often details will be important, especially when you are reading for information.

We looked at *Reading for main ideas* in the first section because it is so much easier to select and remember the details once we recognise the main thought or idea in the writer's mind.

A   *Study the following nine words for one minute:*

potato	turnip	car
dance	lorry	hop
skip	run	bus.

Close your book and write down as many as you can remember.

B   *Study the following nine words for one minute:*

chair	sun	petrol
stool	moon	paraffin
settee	star	diesel.

Close your book and write down as many as you remember.
Did you remember more in B than in A?
Look at both sets of words again.
Why is it more easy to remember the words in B?

C   *Study the following list:*

sole	daisy	banana	cricket
plum	haddock	tulip	hockey
violet	peach	tennis	salmon
flounder	golf	apple	hyacinth.

Before trying to remember the words, think of them under the following headings:

Fish	Flowers	Fruit	Games.

Write down as many of the words as you can remember.
When you know the titles, it is easier to remember the details.

FILL IN THE DETAILS

Read the following passage. Think of a suitable title.

In which direction should he try to escape? The rocks were steep and frightening. To climb them would be quite dangerous, if not impossible, in the dark. Then there was the lake. He was a strong swimmer but before the sun had set he had seen at least one alligator, fierce and forbidding. No doubt there would be others. His only other chance of escape would be through the woods where he knew the enemy would still be lurking silently and unseen. His one hope was to go under cover of darkness, but by which way? In less than two hours dawn would be breaking.

A suitable title might be "Possibilities of escape".

Keeping the title in mind, read the paragraph again and see if you can fill in the details, the three ways by which he could escape. Set your answer out like this:

The paragraph is about "Possibilities of escape".
Details (a) by the r– – –s
      (b) by the l– –e
      (c) through the w– – –s.

Now try the following

The time passed pleasantly enough in a game of advertisements. You know the game, of course. It is something like Dumb Crambo. The players take it in turns to go out, and then come back and look as like some advertisement as they can, and the others have to guess what advertisement it is meant to be. Bobbie came in and sat down under Mother's umbrella and made a sharp face, and everyone knew she was the fox who sits under the umbrella in the advertisement. Phyllis tried to make a Magic Carpet of Mother's waterproof, but it would not stand out stiff and raft-like as a Magic Carpet should, and nobody could guess it. Everyone thought Peter was carrying things a little too far when he blacked his face all over with coal-dust and struck a spidery attitude and said he was the blot that advertises somebody's Blue Black Writing Fluid.

                                (*The Railway Children* – E. Nesbit)

Main idea   Game of advertisements
Details   *(a)*   *(b)*   *(c)*

Read all four paragraphs below.

Then read paragraph 1 carefully and answer the questions on it. Do the same with paragraphs 2, 3 and 4.

1. For a long time men and boys from Newfoundland took part in the annual seal hunt. Although it was a most dangerous adventure there had been a seal hunt every spring for over a hundred years and many turned out. Some had much experience while others had never been before, but the main requirement was that they had to be physically fit.

2. Many a strong and hardy man never returned. Some went down in the icy waters as icebergs smashed their ships. Others disappeared as their boats were driven away by blizzards, and you can imagine the fate of their comrades left behind on the ice floes.

3. Those who survived enjoyed no comfort or luxury. As they had no way of cooking meals, for long spells they had to make do with biscuits and tea which they made from water which itself smelt of seal fat. They slept in the ship's holds without any bedding. And as more and more seal skins were stored aboard, the space for the men became less and less.

4. How they must have longed for present-day conditions. They never lived to see the modern ships in which the crews have warm clothing to wear, comfortable beds to sleep in, three hot meals a day and free medical treatment when sick or injured.

Paragraph 1 is about *the Newfoundland seal hunt.*
Can you fill in the details?
   (a) Who went on it?
   (b) How often did it take place?
   (c) How many years did it last?
   (d) What type of person went?

Paragraph 2 tells us *how men were lost*
Can you fill in the details?
   (a)   *(b)*   *(c)*

Paragraph 3 tells us about *hardships*
   Fill in the details   *(a)*   *(b)*   *(c)*

Paragraph 4 tells us about *advantages today*
   Fill in the details   *(a)*   *(b)*   *(c)*   *(d)*

Landing seals in about the year 1900 in St John's, Newfoundland.

Now see if you can find the main idea and the details.
Remember to write the main idea first.

Bill was not sleeping well. In fright he switched on his light
to see if there was really a burglar in his room or whether it
was part of his dream. There was no one there and not a
sound. As he dozed off again he was the guardsman in scarlet
jacket at the camp gate. When he heard an intruder creep up
behind him he swung round so violently that he woke up
wondering why he was so restless. But he was so tired that he
forgot his fears and was soon gliding on skis down the snow-
clad slopes of the Alps, when the noise of the avalanche woke
him up again. Why so many bad dreams?

Main idea?
   Details (a)   (b)   (c)

Why the disturbed sleep? Could the cheese he had eaten at
suppertime really give him nightmares? Or could it have
been the television programme? But it had been funny and
enjoyable. It could not be the noise of the wind, rain and hail
because that had died down hours ago. And then suddenly he
held his breath and listened. There was something, or
someone, scratching beneath the bed.

Main idea?
   Details (a)   (b)   (c)   (d)

As I was so sitting and thinking, a sound of men and horses came to me through the wood; and presently after, at a turning of the road, I saw four travellers come into view. The way was in this part so rough and narrow that they came single and led their horses by the reins. The first was a great red-headed gentleman, who carried his hat in his hand and fanned himself, for he was in a breathing heat. The second, by his decent black garb and white wig, I correctly took to be a lawyer. The third was a servant, and wore some part of his clothes in tartan, which showed that his master was of a Highland family, and either an outlaw or else in singular good odour with the Government, since the wearing of tartan was against the Act. As for the fourth, who brought up the tail, I had seen his like before, and knew him at once to be a sheriff's officer.

(*Kidnapped*–Robert Louis Stevenson)

A suitable title for the paragraph would be?
   Details (a)   (b)   (c)   (d)

Once stripped, some would jump in recklessly from the side of the pond without even testing the water with an exploratory toe. Others cautiously descended the three or four steps at the shallow end and then gently lowered themselves into the water. A few compromised, and stood on the top step at the shallow end and "scooshed" forward, with tremendous squealing from everyone in their path as the water drenched them.

(*Shoes were for Sunday* – Molly Weir)

Main idea?
   Details (a)   (b)   (c)

Would we find any human still living on the island? We tried the old dilapidated houses one by one. Seven had no roofs, doors or windows and the grey stone walls looked ready to collapse before the violent blasts of the next winter. The eighth house was more complete with its corrugated iron roof, boarded up windows and closed door but no one had lived there for many a day. It seemed to be used for a shelter for sheep or cattle, but today it contained nothing but the remains of a dead sheep, and the smell of rotting plants, flesh and farmyard manure. The last house stood intact. This appeared to have been the school around which children once played happily when they escaped from their lessons. A television aerial suggested someone might be in residence, but no one answered the door. Only our knocking broke the eerie silence behind the shuttered windows.

The main topic in this passage is?
   Details (a)   (b)   (c)

There was life on the island, however. The sea birds hovered above us, screeched as if to sound a warning of intruders and swept over the edge of the cliffs. Rabbits appeared in their scores but only for a fleeting moment before each scampered for cover and safety. The sheep continued to eat the grass beside the path which perhaps was once the main road through this tiny remote kingdom. On the other sides of fences cattle came to investigate. The unfriendly attitude of the cattle, and the menacing look of the bull, urged us to be on our way. As we discussed our gratitude for the protection of fences, David remarked that the newness of the wire indicated the work of someone who had been there recently.

The main topic in this passage is?
   Details (a)   (b)   (c)   .   (d)

William was not slow to realise the danger he was in. Not a stone on the rough track from the shore to the islet could be seen above water. He could try to wade across to the other side, but doubtless that had been what Jerry Mitchell tried to do on that sad day he had heard his parents talk about. Anyhow he saw no easy way of judging the depth of the water or the strength of the current. It would be about another hour before the sun disappeared over the horizon. Would anyone spot him? If only he had told Tommy or David where he was going, someone would have known where to look.

Main idea?
  Details   (a)   (b)   (d)   (d)

William had always been considered a very clever boy. His headmaster often said he was one of the brightest pupils in the school. Last year at the circus he had beaten the Guesser and solved the Circle Puzzle. He had even appeared on television when he demonstrated his own toy motorboat which was powered by the works of an alarm clock. But this was no time to think about such things. His problem was to be clever enough now.

Main idea?
  Details   (a)   (b)   (c)

Councillor Smith:	The time has come for decision. Can we or can we not have a new swimming pool for our young citizens? What are the main problems?
Councillor Edwards:	The main problem is to raise the money. How can we afford it when we need extra finance for house-building and for a new link road?
Treasurer:	The money can be raised. Of course it will mean extra borrowing but it can be done. We can find the money. But where can we build it?
Councillor Dickson:	There is a site in Great Junction Street. If we can raise the money, I see no obstacle in the way of obtaining the site. But if we build the pool will the young people make use of it?
Councillor Jack:	Of course they will. Already groups of them travel the eight kilometres to the Eden Pool every week, and this is because we have not built the pool here which we should have built years ago.
Councillor Smith:	So the question is straightforward. Should we build a swimming pool?

Main idea?
  Details (a)   (b)   (c)

No matter what type of holiday you are looking for you will find the answer in Switzerland. There is really no other country quite like it, for here you have some of the finest and most spectacular scenery in the whole of Europe together with an attractive climate, hotels that have become a byword for comfort and service, and the friendliest and most hospitable people you could wish to meet.

(*Holidays in Switzerland, 1976* – Swiss Travel Service)

Main idea?
  Details   *(a)*   *(b)*   *(c)*   *(d)*

Think of the variety of attractions. You may seek outdoor sporting activities. Walking, swimming, riding, sailing and golf are just a few of the many possibilities for enjoying your holiday. Then there is an infinite variety of excursions by coach, cable car or mountain railway, leisurely afternoons on a lake steamer, historic cities, picturesque castles, music festivals – these are just a few more of the variety of interests for your holiday in Switzerland. In the evening music fills the air, whether it be the local village band or an internationally known orchestra at the Casino, an all star variety show, traditional Swiss folklore entertainment, or a local accordionist as you enjoy your "fondue" in a village inn.

(*Holidays in Switzerland, 1976* – Swiss Travel Service)

Main idea?
  Details   *(a)*   *(b)*   *(c)*   *Grisons, Switzerland*

TRUE OR FALSE?

Here is a different way of finding out how carefully you study details. You have to decide from reading passages whether statements are *True* or *False* or whether the writer *Doesn't say.*

Below are four statements. After each one you see T F and DS. T stands for true, *F stands for* false *and DS stands for* doesn't say. *First of all read over the four statements.*

(1)	David Thom rode White Streak.	T F DS
(2)	He was pleased when Carolina was declared the winner.	T F DS
(3)	The judges were planning to disqualify David.	T F DS
(4)	The winner was David's friend.	F F DS

Now read the passage carefully and in each case write T if the statement is true, F if it is false, and DS if the passage does not mention it.

David Thom, the rider of White Streak, was so sure his horse had won the race that he was annoyed to hear Carolina declared the winner. He dismounted and hurried to the judges to make a strong protest although he knew they could disqualify anyone who did not accept their decision as final.

The chief judge explained that the horses had crossed the line so close together that they could not decide which was first until they received photographs of the finish. The picture showed Carolina winning by a nose.

David apologised and went to congratulate the winner.

Now check your answers.
For (1) you most likely answered T. If not, look at line 1 in the passage. For (2) the answer is F because line 2 says David was "annoyed". For (3) we would answer DS because, although line 4 says the judges "could disqualify" him the passage does not say they were planning to disqualify him. The answer to (4) is DS because we are not actually told whether David was a friend of the winner.

For five years the main street had grown more and more congested with motor cars, making parking more difficult even in side streets in the middle of the town.

It seemed possible that traffic would gradually become very slow-moving, perhaps slower than walking speed. If that happened, car owners might feel it advisable to leave their cars on the outskirts of the town and travel in by bus.

At that time few foresaw the decision of the local Council. Last year they declared the street a pedestrian precinct. On February 1st it was closed to all motor traffic and now the pedestrian walks through it unmolested by the motor car.

Here are 3 statements. From your reading of the passage above, decide whether each one is true (T), false (F), or the passage does not say (DS). Remember to read and study the passage very carefully before you answer.

(1) It was difficult to park in side streets.
(2) Many were fined for parking offences.
(3) Cars are not now allowed on the main street.

Here are five statements.

(1) There are lakes of oil deep underground.
(2) One would have needed a microscope to see the sea creatures.
(3) The sea creatures rotted down in three million years.
(4) The oil rig had been damaged by a 145 kilometre an hour gale.
(5) Scientists cannot guarantee that oil will be found.

From your careful reading of the following passage, decide whether each statement is true (T), false (F), or the passage doesn't say (DS).

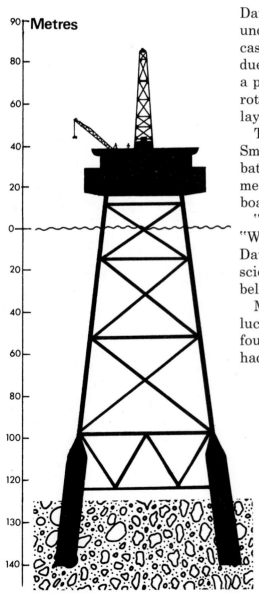

Metres

David had always believed that there are lakes of oil deep underground, but Mr. Smith explained that this is not the case. Countless tiny creatures once lived in seas which in due course became filled in with sand, mud and pebbles. Over a period of millions of years the bodies of those creatures rotted down and are now found as oil and gas within the layers of rocks which were formed.

To David the oil rig seemed huge and very strong. Mr. Smith told him that it had to be strong as it was sometimes battered by winds of over 145 k.p.h. and waves at least 15 metres high. It had to be big because scores of men lived on board and a great deal of heavy equipment was used.

"How do you know where to drill for oil?" asked David. "Well," said Mr. Smith, "seismatic soundings are taken." To David that meant little, but as he listened he gathered that scientists use sound waves to detect whether the rocks down below are likely to contain oil in some of their layers.

Mr. Smith added that it was also very much a matter of luck. Many exploratory holes have been drilled and no oil found, either because there was never any oil there at all or it had already escaped through cracks in the rock formation.

Read over these six statements.

(1) The writer hopes the treasure is never found.
(2) A galleon lies near Tobermory pier.
(3) It is well known how much gold is in the treasure chest.
(4) Some bits of wood have been brought up.
(5) The old Spanish coins which were brought up were valuable.
(6) The writer watched the treasure hunters at work.

Now read the passage below very carefully and decide whether each of the six statements is true (T) or false (F) or whether the writer doesn't say (DS).

I wish someone would find the treasure chest of the Tobermory galleon. Then we might know the truth of this mystery. Does it in fact exist?

There is sufficient evidence that a Spanish galleon lies near Tobermory pier. The claim that it contained vast quantities of gold is not so certain. If it was, why are there so many different estimates of its value, anything from three to thirty million pounds?

The hopeful treasure hunters think there is at least some gold. This year they came full of hope and confidence. With the assistance of their divers, dredgers and expensive equipment they brought up a few old Spanish coins and bits of the ship's timbers. But the treasure chest eluded them all.

Thanksgiving scroll before unrolling.

Arabs searching for scrolls in a Qumran cave.

Here are seven statements.

(1) The writer was on holiday in July.
(2) The writer enjoyed his holiday.
(3) None of the group of travellers sank in the Dead Sea.
(4) He felt nervous in the cable car.
(5) Saul often visited Massada.
(6) The Dead Sea Scrolls were about 2 000 years old.
(7) The Bedu discovered them by accident.

From your very careful reading of the passage decide whether each statement is true (T) or false (F) or whether the writer doesn't say (DS).

My friends must have been envious of me enjoying my first ever winter holiday far away in the Holy Land. I would have so much to tell them when I came back from this glorious land of sunshine and relaxation.

Ari said that the Dead Sea was the most fascinating place on earth, although he admitted later that he had never set foot in any other country. But to me it was fabulous. For long spells I just basked in the sun and gazed out over the Sea. According to the map it is 365 metres below the level of most of the world's other seas, but I did not believe Ari, in spite of his assurances, that people could not sink in it. There was only one way to find out. In I went for a dip and all I did was to float. The same applied to all the others.

From there we went to Massada, 730 metres high and very dry indeed. As the cable car whisked us to the top I wondered if the climb was as difficult as it looked. I did not try to find out. On the top we saw the remains of Herod's ancient palace and fortifications. This was where he stayed every winter.

A few kilometres to the north is Ein Gedi, a delightful oasis in the desert. Its name I remembered from my reading of the Bible. Surely it appeared as beautiful to David long ago when he hid there to avoid Saul who was in close pursuit.

We did not have much farther to travel to find the Qumran Caves where the 2 000 year old Dead Sea Scrolls were found. I pictured the joy of the Bedu who first set eyes on them. Would he have realised there and then that by chance he had stumbled on a valuable treasure?

3. All in order
Alphabetical sequence

FIRST LETTER

a b c d e f g h i j k l m n o p q r s t u v w x y z

Here are four words: *kick, ball, score, goal.*
How do we put them into their correct alphabetical order?
The first letter in each word is different: *k*ick, *b*all, *s*core, *g*oal.
The order in which these letters occur in the alphabet is
(1) *b* (2) *g* (3) *k* (4) *s.*
We put our four words into the order in which the first letters
occur in the alphabet: (1) *ball*, (2) *goal*, (3) *kick*, (4) *score.*

When you consult a dictionary, index, etc., you must be able to recognise alphabetical order. Below are a few opportunities for you to practise this skill.

Now write in alphabetical order the words in each of the following groups. Number each word as you write it.

The word to put first is underlined.

---

1. (a) spaceman, rocket, <u>moon</u>
   (b) knee, <u>ankle</u>, foot
   (c) chair, <u>bed</u>, table, stool

   (d) Indian, gun, <u>boy</u>, tent
   (e) fall, <u>down</u>, hurt, leg
   (f) puncture, <u>car</u>, garage, repair

   (g) milk, goat, <u>butter</u>, cream
   (h) <u>girl</u>, needle, thread, sewing

---

2. (a) referee, whistle, <u>foul</u>, penalty
   (b) sound, fright, darkness, <u>bat</u>, wings
   (c) tree, climb, <u>apples</u>, leg, hurt

   (d) practice, trainer, horse, <u>cup</u>, win
   (e) <u>cat</u>, mouse, loft, scramble, escape
   (f) plane, height, view, <u>fields</u>, towns

   (g) seeds, plants, flowers, lettuces, roses, <u>dahlias</u>
   (h) holiday, <u>beach</u>, sun, dive, cricket, tan

---

3. (a) sound, fright, hole, mouse, trap, <u>cheese</u>
   (b) kite, wind, string, long, <u>break</u>, smash
   (c) sunny, evening, neighbouring, hill, day, <u>chase</u>, rabbit, jumped, found

   (d) guitar, song, play, friends, <u>applause</u>, band
   (e) school, holiday, line, fish, river, kitchen, mother, <u>chips</u>

   (f) tooth, sore, dentist, <u>appointment</u>, filling, relief, chocolate, brush, paste

SECOND LETTER

In the following the first letters of the words are the same. To put these words in alphabetical order we have to look at the *second* letter.

Example: A*l*an, a*t*e, a*n*other, a*p*ple

Correct order: (1) *Alan*, (2) *another*, (3) *apple*, (4) *ate*.

Now do the following. The word to put first is underlined. Number each word as you write it down.

4. (a) boy, broke, <u>bat</u>

(b) inside, <u>ice</u>, island

(c) clever, <u>child</u>, colour, create

(d) <u>jam</u>, junk, jet, job

(e) design, <u>day</u>, domino, distress, drums

(f) knee, kick, keep, kraal, <u>kangaroo</u>

(g) explain, edge, elephant, embark, <u>eager</u>, egg

(h) library, <u>length</u>, lady, lonely, lyre, lamp

5. (a) friend, foul, first, flock, fun, <u>father</u>, feed
   (b) nurse, nobody, neck, <u>narrow</u>, night
   (c) gift, glass, <u>gallop</u>, gnaw, geese, gold, grain
   (d) outside, often, orange, odd, oppress, oil, <u>oasis</u>
   (e) holly, head, hide, hunt, <u>hand</u>, hydrant
   (f) person, picture, prince, <u>parade</u>, plumber, poor, pupil

34

THIRD LETTER

In the following exercises the first two letters of all the words in each group are the same. To put these words in alphabetical order we have to look at the third letter.
Example: in*f*ant, in*c*h, in*s*ist, in*d*eed.
Correct order: (1) *inch*, (2) *indeed*, (3) *infant*, (4) *insist*.

Now do the following in the same way. Number each word as you write it. The first word in each group in 6 and 7 is underlined for you.

6. (a) jumble, juice, <u>juggle</u>
   (b) <u>rail</u>, ration, ramble
   (c) king, kirk, <u>kilt</u>, kite
   (d) sandwich, sage, salmon, <u>saccharine</u>
   (e) lamp, <u>labour</u>, lake, land
   (f) talk, tartan, <u>take</u>, tame
   (g) undo, unfair, <u>unaware</u>, unrest
   (h) village, vinegar, <u>view</u>, vixen

7. (a) wall, waist, <u>waddle</u>, warn, wander
   (b) comet, coffee, cold, <u>cod</u>, coil
   (c) fall, fail, <u>face</u>, fan, fag, famous
   (d) <u>glad</u>, glide, glum, glee, gloss, glycerine
   (e) nothing, <u>nobody</u>, nose, nod, nonsense, noise
   (f) trust, troops, trench, <u>trap</u>, trim, try

35

8. Example: unkind   Correct order: (1) under
        unwell   (2) unkind
        under   (3) unrest
        unrest   (4) unwell

Now do the following.
Number the words as you write them down.

(a)	(b)	(c)
open	code	make
oppose	coffee	mail
opinion	cocoa	magnify
opal	coal	man
option	coin	macaroni
	colour	mask

(d)	(e)	(f)
distance	numb	excess
dizzy	nuisance	exhibit
ditch	nurse	explore
divert	nudge	example
diet	nun	exit
dice	nut	extension

(g) pan
    pad
    page
    pale
    pace
    pail
    paper
    pamphlet

4. Read with speed
Skimming

When you were reading for detail, you found you had to read slowly. There were many thoughts you had to study and understand. The more difficult the section, the more slowly you had to read.

You often come across easy sections which you can read quickly. If you are looking for one special word and the rest is of no interest to you, then you move your eyes very rapidly over the print. You are not reading all the words carefully. This skill of glancing over material rapidly is called *skimming*

Some types of skimming are more rapid than others. Perhaps the most rapid of all occurs when you try to find a word in a list.

USING AN INDEX

You are now going to practise skimming.

First of all, in your own book make a copy of the answer column on the right hand side of this page (below).

Imagine you have a book about sports and wish to find out about some of them.

Look at each question and see which sport is mentioned.
The index opposite tells you which page you should refer to.
Keep the name of the sport in mind and glance rapidly down the index until you find it.
Write out in your own answer column the number of the page you should refer to. See how quickly you can find each one.

A1 and B1 are done for you.

A	If you wish to find out:	Answer Column	
(1)	information about <u>golf</u> clubs	(1)	32
(2)	the length of the course in a <u>marathon</u>	(2)	
(3)	the number of players in a <u>netball</u> team	(3)	
(4)	how to hold a <u>javelin</u>	(4)	
(5)	different strokes in <u>swimming</u>	(5)	
(6)	the equipment you require for <u>ski-ing</u>	(6)	
(7)	how to score in <u>lacrosse</u>	(7)	
(8)	different ways of <u>diving</u>	(8)	
(9)	the rules of <u>badminton</u>	(9)	
(10)	the events in the <u>pentathlon</u>	(10)	

B	If you wish to find out:		
(1)	how to throw the hammer	(1)	8
(2)	the distances between hurdles	(2)	
(3)	sizes of football pitches	(3)	
(4)	how to balance a canoe	(4)	
(5)	the best footwear for sprinting	(5)	
(6)	types of tracks used for cycling	(6)	
(7)	the kind of racquet you need for squash	(7)	
(8)	the height of a volleyball net	(8)	
(9)	how to keep the score in cricket	(9)	
(10)	how to fall in judo	(10)	

Make a copy of the answer columns.
Read the question. Refer to the index opposite.
Write out the number of the page on which you can read about
the flower mentioned. Number 1 in each exercise is done for
you. Check that it is correct.
Work very quickly.

A You can read about   on page
   (1) iris   (1)   4
   (2) phlox   (2)
   (3) geum   (3)
   (4) wallflower   (4)
   (5) orchid   (5)

B You can read about   on page
   (1) hyacinth   (1) 33
   (2) stocks   (2)
   (3) echeveria   (3)
   (4) bulbs   (4)
   (5) pyrethrum   (5)
   (6) viola   (6)

C You can read about   on page
   (1) dahlia   (1) 42
   (2) poppy   (2)
   (3) xeranthemum (3)
   (4) salvia   (4)
   (5) marguerite   (5)
   (6) carnation   (6)
   (7) larkspur   (7)

D You can read about   on page
   (1) freesia   (1) 39, 54
   (2) jasmine   (2)
   (3) antirrhinum   (3)
   (4) pansy   (4)
   (5) sunflower   (5)
   (6) primula   (6)
   (7) nasturtium   (7)
   (8) ursinia   (8)

Refer to the index opposite.
Write out the correct number of the page on which you can
read about each item.
Number 1 is done for you in each exercise. Check to see if it is
correct.

A You can read about	on page	B You can read about	on page
(1) airship	(1) 36	(1) gates	(1) 82
(2) aircraft	(2)	(2) enemy	(2)
(3) brakes	(3)	(3) Concorde	(3)
(4) camouflage	(4)	(4) exhibition	(4)
(5) buffet	(5)	(5) chromium	(5)
		(6) aerodrome	(6)

C You can read about	on page	D You can read about	on page
(1) carburettor	(1) 6	(1) centigrade	(1) 69
(2) enemy	(2)	(2) runway	(2)
(3) levers	(3)	(3) nuclear power	(3)
(4) improvements	(4)	(4) iron	(4)
(5) kits	(5)	(5) demonstration	(5)
(6) compass	(6)	(6) longitude	(6)
		(7) fashion	(7)

E You can read about	on page	F You can read about	on page
(1) BAC 1-11	(1) 27	(1) speed	(1) 79
(2) uniform	(2)	(2) log	(2)
(3) jet	(3)	(3) enemy	(3)
(4) machine	(4)	(4) Zeppelin	(4)
(5) gangway	(5)	(5) implement	(5)
(6) pump	(6)	(6) wreck	(6)
(7) Heron	(7)	(7) diameter	(7)
(8) torpedo	(8)	(8) licence	(8)
(9) diary	(9)	(9) wind	(9)
(10) radar	(10)	(10) loop-the-loop	(10)
(11) gyration	(11)	(11) yo-yo	(11)

On the opposite page you will see an atlas index. For each entry you are given

		Example
(i)	the name of the place	Aberdeen
(ii)	the country where it is situated,	Scotland
(iii)	the page of the atlas on which to find the map,	16
(iv)	the area of the map in which you will find the place.	D3

Refer to the index page and write out the correct number of the page in the atlas on which you will find the map containing each of the following places.

A 1. Cuba 71
  2. Hailun
  3. Mainz
  4. Peru
  5. Ussel

B 1. Yeovil
  2. Dundee
  3. Kariba
  4. Martinique
  5. Falun

Write out the correct page number of the atlas and also the area of the map where you will find each of the following places:

C 1. Laval 33 B2
  2. Usk
  3. Ramelton
  4. Parana
  5. Epsom
  6. Mainz

D 1. Zetland
  2. Reefton
  3. Hesse
  4. Bordeaux
  5. Andes, mts.
  6. Gallipoli

E *Write the correct page number of the atlas where you will find each of the following countries:*

1. England 17
2. China
3. France
4. Japan
5. Sweden
6. Turkey
7. West Germany
8. West Indies
9. Zambia

F *Write down the number of places mentioned in the index which are in each of the following countries:*

1. France 6
2. Argentina
3. Spain
4. Sweden
5. Greece
6. Scotland
7. Eire
8. USA
9. USSR
10. South America

Extracted from an atlas index

Aberdeen	Scotland	16	D3	Negro, R.	Argentina	73	D11
Alabama, state	USA	65	J4	Noshiro	Japan	51	O3
Andes, mts.	S America	72	B4	Ob, R.	USSR	46	G2
Baku	USSR	46	E4	Orange	France	33	D4
Bordeaux	France	33	B4	Oxford	England	17	E6
Chatham	England	17	F6	Parana	Argentina	73	E10
Cuba	W Indies	71	H3	Peru	S America	72	B6
Dundee	Scotland	16	D3	Puerto Rico, I.	W Indies	71	L4
Dusseldorf	W Germany	34	B3	Quimper	France	33	A2
Elista	USSR	46	E4	Ramelton	Eire	30	D2
Epsom	England	17	E6	Reefton	New Zealand	79	C5
Esquel	Argentina	73	C12	Rumoi	Japan	51	P3
Falun	Sweden	42	C3	Salto	Argentina	73	F10
Feira	Zambia	59	D2	Scalloway	Scotland	16	E1
Flannan Is.	Scotland	16	B2	Taishun	China	51	K6
Gallipoli	Turkey	39	G4	Tottori	Japan	51	N4
Gironde R.	France	33	B4	Tynemouth	England	17	E4
Hailun	China	51	M2	Usk	Wales	26	E3
Hesse	W Germany	34	B4	Ussel	France	33	C4
Illinois, state	USA	65	H2	Valencia	Spain	36	D3
Iona, I.	Scotland	16	B3	Volos	Greece	39	F5
Izhevsk	USSR	46	F3	Wellington	New Zealand	79	E4
Jorn	Sweden	42	E2	Wesel	W Germany	34	B3
Julianstown	Eire	30	E4	Whitchurch	Wales	26	E2
Kailu	China	51	L3	Xanthe	Greece	39	G4
Kariba	Zambia	59	C2	Yeovil	England	17	D6
Laval	France	33	B2	Yingtan	China	51	J6
Lumsden	New Zealand	79	B6	Zetland	Scotland	16	E1
Mainz	W Germany	34	B4				
Martinique	W Indies	71	M5				

Andrews	Mary V.	10 White Street	018-416-3402
Baker	James	84 Manor Drive	018-416-5116
Carnegie	Mrs N. M.	31 Main Road	018-442-3007
Dewar	Dr George	50 High Street	018-416-2443
Ferguson	Fiona Y.	63 Bridge Crescent	Lestin 612
Munro	David	7A East Road	018-416-3556
Oliver	John C.	14 Bridge Grove	Lestin 228

TELEPHONE DIRECTORY

Read the question and refer to the telephone directory above.

See how quickly you can spot which of the suggested answers is the correct one to complete the sentence. (The key word or number is underlined for you.)
Write the letter only (not the whole answer) in each case. The answer to the first one would be written 1 (d).

1. *Dr Dewar lives in*
   (a) Manor Drive; (b) Bridge Crescent; (c) Kirk Avenue; (d) High Street

2. *018 416 5116 is the 'phone number of*
   (a) John Oliver; (b) Fiona Ferguson; (c) Mrs Carnegie; (d) James Baker

3. *One of the people who lives in Lestin is*
   (a) James Baker; (b) David Munro; (c) Fiona Ferguson; (d) Mary Andrews

---

Read the question and spot the answer quickly on the Telephone Directory opposite (page 47).

Which of the suggested answers is the correct one? Write the letter only (not the whole answer).

A (1) *Which Yale is listed last?*
   (a) Adam; (b) David; (c) Robert; (d) William
  (2) *What is the Doctor's surname?*
   (a) Yale; (b) Yapp; (c) Yardley; (d) Yates; (e) Yarwood

Yale, Adam E.	4 Main Street	059-452-6321
Yale, David J.	7 George Street	059-421-5213
Yale, Robert	8 Riverside Loan	Dunin 839
Yale, William S.	64 Main Street	059-452-6425
Yapp Furnishings	35 High Street	059-361-2424
Yapp, George F.	4 Albert Street	059-621-3720
Yapp, Margaret	20 Gordon Lane	059-775-3275
Yapp, Peter	3 Grey Avenue	059-668-3624
Yapp Upholstery	36 High Street	059-361-2621
Yardley, Dr Archibald	41 George Street	059-421-5322
Yare Hydraulic Engineering Co	35 Main Street	059-452-5621
Yarwood Restaurant	11 Redford Avenue	Oldham 475
Yarwood, Zena F.	7 High Street	059-361-2728
Yates, Alan S.	18 Spring Gardens	059-668-3829

B (1) *Which Yale lives in Dunin?*
(a) Adam; (b) David; (c) Robert; (d) William
(2) *Who lives in Grey Avenue?*
(a) Alan Yates; (b) Margaret Yapp; (c) Adam Yale; (d) Peter Yapp
(3) *What is the Yarwood Restaurant's telephone number?*
(a) Dunin 839; (b) Oldham 475; (c) 059-452-5621
(4) *In which street would you find a furnishings firm?*
(a) Gordon Lane; (b) Grey Avenue; (c) High Street; (d) Riverside Loan
(5) *Which Yapp is listed first?*
(a) Furnishings; (b) George; (c) Margaret; (d) Peter; (e) Upholstery
(6) *Who lives in Spring Gardens?*
(a) Margaret Yapp; (b) William Yale; (c) George Yapp; (d) Alan Yates
(7) *What is Margaret Yapp's telephone number?*
(a) 6425; (b) 3275; (c) 2728; (d) 2424
(8) *What is the number of Yarwood in High Street?*
(a) 26; (b) 18; (c) 11; (d) 7

TIMETABLES

Local entertainments

Read each question and decide which is the key word to look for.

Skim through the programme of local entertainments (opposite) till you find the key word. Which of the suggested answers is the correct one? Write the letter only. The first one is done for you. Check it.

Answer

1. *Where does boating take place?*
   (a) Ambria; (b) Old Course; (c) Lake Arno; (d) River Durk   1 (c)

2. *On which evening can you go to the cinema?*
   (a) Sunday; (b) Monday; (c) Tuesday; (d) Wednesday

3. *Which entertainment takes place on Old Course?*
   (a) crazy golf; (b) bowling; (c) boating; (d) pony trekking

4. *At what time does crazy golf begin?*
   (a) 1.15 pm; (b) 2 pm; (c) 4.20 pm; (d) 7 pm

5. *Where would you go for the concert?*
   (a) Ambria; (b) Regina; (c) New Gardens; (d) Town Gardens

6. *At what time does bowling start?*
   (a) 1.15 pm; (b) 2 pm; (c) 4.20 pm; (d) 7 pm

7. *Which entertainment takes place in Town Gardens?*
   (a) concert; (b) crazy golf; (c) bowling; (d) pony trekking

8. *Which entertainment can you go to on Fridays?*
   (a) boating; (b) cinema; (c) concert; (d) fishing

Local Entertainments			
Event	Day	Venue	Time
Boating	Tuesday	Lake Arno	3 pm
Bowling	Thursday	New Gardens	2 pm
Cinema	Monday	Ambria	7 pm
Concert	Friday	Regina	8.30 pm
Crazy golf	Saturday	Town Gardens	4.20 pm
Fishing	Sunday	River Durk	1.14 pm
Pony Trekking	Wednesday	Old Course	3.30 pm

Evening Entertainments

See how quickly you can spot the answers to the questions on page 51. (Something is underlined in each question in A. That is what you should look for first of all.)
Which is the correct answer? Write the letter only.

Day	Event	Venue	Time	Admission
Sunday	Football	View Park	4 pm	20p
	Beauty Contest	Bathing pool	8 pm	30p
Monday	Concert	Town Hall	7.30 pm	35p
	Ten-pin bowling	Bowling Alley	10 pm	25p
Tuesday	Indoor Tennis	New Sports Centre	6 pm	40p
	Mystery Tour	Bus Station	8 pm	85p
	Discotheque	Rainbow	10.30 pm	20p
Wednesday	Film Show	Odeon	8.30 pm	40p
	Open Air dancing	Promenade Gardens	10.50 pm	15p
Thursday	Concert	Market Hall	7.30 pm	35p
	Ten-pin bowling	Bowling Alley	10 pm	25p
Friday	Football	South Stadium	6 pm	20p
	Fireworks display	View Park	9 pm	10p
	Discotheque	Rainbow	10.30pm	20p
Saturday	Film Show	Ritz	8.30 pm	50p
	Indoor tennis	New Sports Centre	6 pm	40p

A (1) *Which entertainment starts at 4 pm?*
        (a) ten pin bowling; (b) football; (c) discotheque;
        (d) indoor tennis
    (2) *How many film shows are there in the Odeon?*
        (a) 1; (b) 2; (c) 3; (d) 4
    (3) *Which entertainment starts at 10.30 pm?*
        (a) fireworks display; (b) discotheque; (c) film show;
        (d) open air dancing
    (4) *Which is the dearest entertainment (85p)?*
        (a) film show; (b) indoor tennis; (c) mystery tour; (d)
        concert
    (5) *For which entertainment would you report to the bus
        station?*
        (a) football; (b) indoor tennis; (c) mystery tour; (d)
        discotheque
    (6) *Which is the cheapest entertainment (10p)?*
        (a) open air dancing; (b) football; (c) fireworks
        display; (d) film show
    (7) *What is the price of admission to indoor tennis?*
        (a) 20p; (b) 25p; (c) 30p; (d) 40p
    (8) *How many beauty contests are there during the
        week?*
        (a) 1; (b) 2; (c) 3; (d) 4

B *In the following questions more than one answer may be
   correct. Write the letters only of the correct answers.*
    (1) *At what times do concerts start?*
        (a) 5 pm; (b) 6.15 pm; (c) 7.30 pm; (d) 8 pm; (e) 10
        pm
    (2) *Which entertainments are available for 20p?*
        (a) beauty contest; (b) football; (c) fireworks; (d)
        discotheque; (e) open air dancing
    (3) *Where are film shows held?*
        (a) Rainbow; (b) Market Hall; (c) Odeon; (d) South
        Stadium; (e) Ritz
    (4) *Where are concerts held?*
        (a) View Park; (b) Market Hall; (c) Odeon; (d) Ritz;
        (e) Town Hall
    (5) *On which evenings can you watch indoor tennis?*
        (a) Monday; (b) Tuesday; (c) Wednesday; (d)
        Friday; (e) Saturday
    (6) *Which entertainments take place in View Park?*
        (a) beauty contest; (b) football; (c) mystery tour; (d)
        fireworks display; (e) ten-pin bowling
    (7) *Where is football played?*
        (a) View Park; (b) New Sports Centre; (c) Rainbow;
        (d) South Stadium

Fly to Gabania

July/August	From	Airline	Flight No	Depart	Arrive	Via
Mo	Birmingham	EEA	EE305	1800	2205	Frankfurt
	Manchester	NWA	NW281	0630	1035	Rome
Tu	Glasgow	EEA	EE314	1530	1910	Non-stop
We	Gatwick	RZA	RZ225	1640	1940	Non-stop
	Heathrow	LVA	LV991	1145	1530	Frankfurt
Th	Manchester	NWA	NW623	1000	1405	Munich
Fr	Luton	NWA	NW748	1125	1425	Non-stop
	Birmingham	EEA	EE368	1630	2035	Zurich
Sa	Heathrow	LVA	LV185	0950	1335	Frankfurt
	Glasgow	EEA	EE412	1330	1720	Non-stop

Spot the answer quickly. Write out the correct answer (letter only).

A (1) *Which airline operates from Luton?*
(a) LVA; (b) EEA; (c) RZA; (d) NWA

(2) *On which day does Flight No. NW 748 operate?*
(a) Wednesday; (b) Thursday; (c) Friday; (d) Saturday

(3) *From where does the Wednesday plane via Frankfurt start its journey?*
(a) Manchester; (b) Heathrow; (c) Luton; (d) Glasgow

(4) *If you depart at 11.45 when do you arrive?*
(a) 1530; (b) 1640; (c) 1800; (d) 2205

(5) *On which airline do you fly from Gatwick?*
(a) NWA; (b) RZA; (c) EEA; (d) LVA

(6) *On which day would you land at Zurich?*
(a) Wednesday; (b) Thursday; (c) Friday; (d) Saturday

(7) *On which day can you fly by RZA or LVA?*
(a) Thursday; (b) Wednesday; (c) Tuesday; (d) Friday

B In this section and the next there may be more than one answer.

(1) *From where do EEA planes operate?*
(a) Glasgow; (b) Luton; (c) Birmingham; (d) Manchester

(2) *On which flight can you fly via Rome?*
(a) EE305; (b) EE412; (c) LV185; (d) NW281

(3) *At what time would you depart on the flight via Zurich?*
(a) 06.30; (b) 16.30; (c) 13.30; (d) 15.30

(4) *On how many days can you get a non-stop flight?*
(a) 2; (b) 3; (c) 4; (d) 5

(5) *On which days can you fly from Heathrow?*
(a) Tuesday; (b) Wednesday; (c) Thursday; (d) Friday; (e) Saturday

(6) *On which day do you arrive at 20.35?*
(a) Wednesday; (b) Thursday; (c) Friday; (d) Saturday

C (1) *On which day can you fly non-stop from Luton?*
(a) Wednesday; (b) Thursday; (c) Friday; (d) Saturday

(2) *What are the numbers of the flights which leave from Birmingham?*
(a) EE368; (b) EE314; (c) EE412; (d) EE305

(3) *On which day can you take the 06.30 flight?*
(a) Saturday; (b) Monday; (c) Tuesday; (d) Sunday

(4) *From which airports can you fly non-stop?*
(a) Glasgow; (b) Heathrow; (c) Gatwick; (d) Luton

(5) *From which town can you fly via Zurich?*
(a) Luton; (b) Manchester; (c) Glasgow; (d) Birmingham

(6) *From where could you fly via Frankfurt?*
(a) Heathrow; (b) Manchester; (c) Birmingham; (d) Luton

(7) *At which airport would you get the LV991 flight?*
(a) Luton; (b) Glasgow; (c) Heathrow; (d) Birmingham

(8) *On which airline would you fly from Luton?*
(a) RZA; (b) NWA; (c) LVA; (d) EEA

(9) *LVA flights fly via which airport?*
(a) Munich; (b) Heathrow; (c) Zurich; (d) Rome

KEY POINTS

Here are four sentences.
1. In the evenings he sat beside his coal fire.
2. By day you would often see him salmon fishing in the river.
3. Salmon was his favourite fish.
4. He cooked it himself on the open coal fire.

Now find the sentences which contain the word coal *and the sentences which contain the word* salmon. *Take one word at a time and look through the sentences quickly.* Coal *is mentioned in sentences 1 and 4 and* salmon *in sentences 2 and 3. Write your answers in the following way:*

    Coal   1,4
    Salmon   2,3

Write out the following lists of words in your own book. Take one word at a time and look through the sentences below and opposite under the same letter as the list. (E.g. for words under A, look at sentences in Group A.) Write down the number of each sentence in which you see the word appear. The first one (cycling) is done for you.

A. cycling 3,7	B. television	C. holidays
racing	chocolate	cottage
snow	football	flowers
	birthday	cold
		ice-cream

A (1) Tom and David like snow but could not agree on what to do.
   (2) Ski-ing was impossible because the snow was too wet.
   (3) Cycling is really Tom's favourite sport.
   (4) They would both have preferred Tom's uncle to take them for a run in the racing car, but there was no chance.
   (5) The tracks were completely blocked by snow in places.
   (6) It was so bad they could not even watch the racing cars practising.
   (7) Where could they go cycling in the present conditions?

B (1) Mark likes playing football.
  (2) He will be eleven on his birthday next week.
  (3) Every night he watches television.
  (4) His grandmother is going to give him a chocolate Easter egg.
  (5) For his birthday he will also get a football jersey.
  (6) He does not stay up late to watch television.
  (7) Getting up early gives him time for football in the school playground in the morning.
  (8) After his birthday he hopes to play in the first team.
  (9) The school football championship for this year has been decided.

C (1) The holidays in Spain were over.
  (2) Ann and Margaret had enjoyed themselves very much, although Ann had had a day in bed with a cold.
  (3) Now they were off to join their parents in a cottage.
  (4) It was in a quiet country district with heather and wild flowers in bloom all around.
  (5) Some people thought the cottage too quiet, but Ann and Margaret did not worry.
  (6) They could enjoy holidays almost anywhere.
  (7) They liked the food except for the cottage cheese.
  (8) The weather on the first morning was cold compared to the sunny days in Spain.
  (9) Their pocket money had all been spent, but that did not matter as there was no shop in which to buy anything, such as ice-cream or sweets.
  (10) Unless it became too cold, they would be out and about from early morning till late evening.
  (11) It was very pleasant to look for flowers or berries, go walking, pony-trekking and climbing hills.
  (12) Saturday would come all too soon and that would be the end of their holidays.

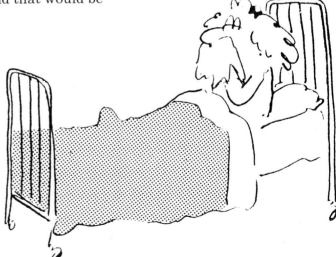

Related words

You have been reading very rapidly (skimming) because you were asked to spot one word (or one group of figures). You will not be able to skim at the same very fast speed when the answer is expressed in a different word or phrase from that used in the question.

For instance, if you are looking for information about *soldiers* in the following list of headings – athletes, cowboys, Indians, pilots, sailors, troops – you notice that the word *soldiers* does not appear but the word *troops* does and it is under this heading you will look for information.

If you are looking for *colour* in this list – box, green, lamp, street, wood – the word *colour* is not in the list, but you see the word *green*, and you know this is a *colour*.

For each word in A write out a word in B which expresses a connected idea.

	A	B
(1)	animal	cycle, hill, horse, music, niece, priest
(2)	circus	candle, clowns, field, lorry, post, street
(3)	furniture	bottle, dial, floor, ink, shoe, table
(4)	game	apple, butter, ears, football, plants, zebra
(5)	house	axe, basket, loaf, pavement, stark, villa
(6)	light	boot, candle, magazine, olive, pencil, stud
(7)	music	darkness, eel, grass, lunch, piano, shadow
(8)	paraffin	bridge, dust, ghost, oil, river, temperature
(9)	remedy	approach, board, cook, cure, intrude, tulip
(10)	vegetable	apron, barrow, district, hostel, potato, spark

Connected ideas

Each item in column 1 needs a phrase from column 2 to make it a more interesting sentence. Take each one in turn from the first column and look rapidly down column 2 for the most suitable phrase. Remember that the ideas in each pair you put together should be connected in some way.

Example: In Group A, 1. begins "The artist painted". We look quickly down the second column and see that (c) "a beautiful picture" will complete the sense. We can write the answer as 1c.

Now do the others the same way.

A 1. The artist painted   (a) on the letter
   2. Alan was reading   (b) in the river
   3. William put a stamp   (c) a beautiful picture
   4. The nurse took   (d) from the launching pad
   5. The rocket rose   (e) his favourite book
   6. Tom liked fishing   (f) the patient's temperature

B 1. The train came to a halt   (a) on her birthday
   2. The lion was hunting   (b) on the wrong runway
   3. Mary was given presents   (c) outside the railway station
   4. The doctor told the patient   (d) in the jungle
   5. The pilot landed the plane   (e) when the team scored a goal
   6. The gardener planted seeds   (f) to stay in bed until she felt better
   7. The football supporters cheered   (g) in the flower beds

C 1. The ship carried   (a) by the fierce gale
   2. Birds were building   (b) in pits far underground
   3. The tree was blown down   (c) a cargo of grain
   4. Many fish were caught   (d) for their bravery in battle
   5. The soldiers were praised   (e) their nests in the trees
   6. The snow was melted   (f) by the heat of the sun
   7. Miners dig coal   (g) in the trawler's nets

D 1. The fireman sprayed foam   (a) her new coat and hat

2. The mountaineer enjoyed   (b) a very fast race

3. Mary was singing   (c) on the blazing fire
4. Every athlete ran   (d) legs and feet ache
5. He found a purse   (e) climbing to great heights
6. The long hard walk made   (f) her favourite song

7. Jane was wearing   (g) which contained some money

Each idea in the first column is expressed in a different way somewhere in the second column. Different words are used. Try to match each pair which expresses one idea.
Example: 1 (d)

A 1. The conquest of Mount Everest   (a) Holiday makers start their sea cruise

2. The story of fireworks   (b) James and John head for the moon

3. The sailing of the *QE2*   (c) How squibs have been developed throughout the years

4. The war of independence   (d) Mountaineers on the summit of the world

5. Journey into space   (e) The fight for freedom
6. Land transport throughout the ages   (f) Don't allow animals to disappear

7. Protection of wild life   (g) How vehicles have improved since the invention of the wheel

B 1. "Learn to swim" week   (a) Fishing dispute in the North Sea

2. History of flight   (b) Strange objects from outer space

3. Cod War   (c) Man's efforts to become airborne

4. Mystery of flying saucers   (d) Safety in the water

5. Increase in the price of meat   (e) Afford a quick trip to America

6. Cheap flights across the North Atlantic   (f) Treat the bodywork of your car

7. New protection against rust   (g) Dearer food

Find the meaning

*In the following passages all unimportant words are left out.
See how much meaning you can get from skimming through
the words left. (<u>No</u> and <u>not</u> are very important words.)*

A. ____ Mr Gray read ____ farmer __ Canada ____ cheap
electricity ____ _ wind generator, __ thought ____ __ ____
use __ wind ____ cheap electricity ____ country cottage.
__ __ ____ __ erected _ windmill ___ _____ _
generator, both __ ____ ____ ____ expensive. __ ___ many
other things __ buy __ much work ____ before __ ____ ____
__ ___ electric light.
        __ ____ _ could not condemn __ oil lamps. _____ long
calm spells __ __ no electric light. __ soon _____ realise
___ _ __ spent _ lot __ money __ ____ __ __ _____
unreliable _____ _ electricity. __ wondered __ _ ____ ____
____ wiser __ ____ allowed __ Electricity Board __ connect
__ supply ____ cottage.

In the summary below which words have been missed out?

Mr Gray thought that electricity generated by wind would
be (1) _____ but the things he had to buy were (2) _____.
During spells of calm weather he had to use (3) _____. In
fact he might have obtained cheaper electricity from the (4)

_____ ____.

_____

B. __ members __ __ Parents' Association __ expected __
____ __ __ money raised before __ school __ ended __
30th June. __ headmaster __ already ____ _ order __ _
microphone __ amplifiers so __ __ ____ use __ ___
closing ceremony.
        __ ___ jumble sale __ not raise __ expected £250 __ __
attendance __ __ coffee morning __ __ disappointing.
Some _____ thought __ money _____ _ borrowed __ __
time being __ others ___ inclined _ __ view ___ __
headmaster _____ cancel __ order.

Which words are missing in the summary below?

The money was to have been raised before the (1) __ of the
school session. The sale raised (2) ___ than £250. Some
thought the headmaster should (3) _____ money for the
equipment but others thought he should (4) _____ __ ____.

READING FOR INFORMATION

You will very often find that the most efficient way of answering questions on passages is to skim along until you see the information you require. Study the questions and remember all the important words. They will guide you to the answer.

In the questions below all the important words are underlined. Keep them in mind as you skim through the passage to find the answer. Then read it carefully, and after that write the answer.

Turn to page 12.
1. How does a mosquito prevent clotting of human blood?
2. What is the difference between the sting of the bee and that of the wasp?
3. Why are insects a problem in tropical regions?

Turn to pages 16–17.
1. What help was sent from France?
2. Why was Captain Talbot afraid during the voyage from France?
3. How were the sailors lucky on landing?
4. How was the gold taken ashore?

Turn to page 20.
1. What was the main danger from ice-bergs?
2. What sort of meals did the crews have?
3. How are conditions better in modern ships?

Turn to page 32. (Remember that sometimes the answer is expressed in a different word from that in the question.)
1. In which other countries had Ari travelled?
2. What happened when the writer went in for a swim?
3. Where did David hide from Saul?
4. How old are the Dead Sea Scrolls?

5. The reason why
Cause and effect

LINKING CAUSE AND EFFECT

One thing may cause another. For example:
Heavy rains sometimes cause flooding.
Heavy rains are the <u>cause</u>. Flooding is the <u>effect</u>.

Consider the following sentence:
Robert was happy because he had received a present.
What was the <u>cause</u>? (Ask yourself, "Why?") "because he had received a present".

What was the <u>effect</u>?
"Robert was happy".

In the following (1-5) the cause and effect are given as separate sentences in each case.
Join each pair together and write as one sentence. Use joining words such as: <u>because</u>, <u>since</u>, <u>as</u>, *etc.*

<u>EFFECT</u>	<u>CAUSE</u> (Why?)
1. There was a holiday from school.	It was the Queen's birthday.
2. He went out to play golf.	The weather forecast was good.
3. The bushes withered.	He had applied weed killer by mistake.
4. The journey took three hours.	There was heavy traffic on the roads.
5. Alfred hoped for snow.	He enjoyed ski-ing.

The following sentence is divided into 2 parts (a) and (b).

1. (a) The team played well (b) because they had been promised a reward.

   What was the cause? (Remember to ask yourself, "Why?") .... (b)
   What was the effect? .... (a)

To save writing out both parts of the sentence we might write our answers as follows:

CAUSE   EFFECT
1. (b)   (a)

Now do the same for sentences numbered 2 to 6.
2. (a) George stayed in bed (b) because he had a cold.
3. (a) Jane switched on the television (b) since it was time for her favourite programme.
4. (a) As it was a school holiday (b) the boys went swimming.
5. (a) Because he did not like school lunches (b) William took a packed lunch to school.
6. (a) Mary joined the choir (b) because she liked singing.

In column 1 we have a list of causes and in column 2 a list of effects.

In 1 the *cause* is "Charles was going on a cruise". Look through the second column and find the *effect* which would match it. Obviously it is E "He went aboard the ship". (The ideas in 1 and E are connected.)

We can record our answer as follows: 1 E.

Now do the others in the same way.

CAUSE	EFFECT
1. Charles was going on a cruise.	A. She received the prize.
2. It was too hot in the room.	B. He was kicking a tin.
3. Grace sang the best solo.	C. He is very fit.
4. Andrew could not find a ball.	D. David switched on the fan.
5. The petrol tank was empty.	E. He went aboard the ship.
6. John takes exercise every day.	F. The car would not start.

Alexander the Great

Short sentences are written below in pairs. One states the cause, the other the effect.
After studying the passage on the next page decide which is which.
The first one is done for you.

1. (a) The horse threw the servants. (Cause)
   (b) The servants were very frightened. (Effect)

2. (a) Alexander was very confident.
   (b) Philip allowed Alexander to ride the horse.

3. (a) Some hoped Alexander would be thrown.
   (b) Alexander was very proud.

4. (a) The shadow might be frightening the horse.
   (b) Alexander kept the horse facing the sun.

5. (a) Philip was pleased.
   (b) Philip gave Alexander the horse.

6. (a) Alexander was proud of the horse.
   (b) A city was named Bucephala.

Some expected Alexander would be the greatest king of all. Others thought he would be a fearless leader in battle as they already saw signs of remarkable courage and confidence while he was still a boy.

One day he and his father, King Philip, were watching the attempts of some royal servants to tame a wild horse. As each man in turn mounted, the horse had reared, kicked, and roared furiously. In a few seconds the rider was thrown into the air and landed on the ground, shaken and frightened.

When there were few volunteers left, Alexander asked his father for permission to prove he could do it. The King was reluctant to allow the young Prince as he feared he might be injured or even killed. But Alexander looked so fearless and sure of success that Philip relented.

Some of the crowd standing around secretly hoped that the boy's pride would receive a blow, but he calmly mounted the horse and rode away.

He had studied what happened in the case of each previous rider. Something was frightening the horse each time. It occurred to him, "Could it be its own shadow which might appear to the horse as a dark moving object?" He kept the horse facing the sun and rode away without incident.

Alexander's father was so pleased that he told him to keep the horse for his own. Alexander named it Bucephalus. It became famous as the horse that carried Alexander through many battles as he built his mighty empire. So great was King Alexander's attachment to the horse that, when it died, he named a city "Bucephala" in its honour.

The new school

Magnus felt very strange in the new school. As a building it was so very small compared to his London school and there were so few pupils that the teacher seemed to be able to keep her eye on him all the time.

At lunch time they were locked out for an hour and a half, no doubt because the teacher had no one to supervise them when she was at lunch. Often it was very cold in the playground shelter as it had no doors on the front.

Yet there were things Magnus liked. The playground was so big that there was plenty of room for everyone to play. They could play football when they wished but could never have a good team with only eight boys altogether. In the mornings he could walk the short distance and have no worries about late buses.

His biggest problem was the dialect his friends talked in the playground. He could understand them in the classroom when they spoke in English. Once they were outside they seemed to speak a different language, and how they all laughed when he tried to speak it!

Match the effect *in column 1 with the correct* cause *in column 2*
For example: "Magnus felt unhappy" (because) (e) "he was in a new school", so we could write 1(e). Do the others the same way.

1. Magnus felt unhappy.
2. The teacher could watch him.
3. They did not get into school at lunch time.

4. They did not have a good team.
5. He walked to school.

6. The boys were amused.

(a) The teacher was away
(b) The distance was short

(c) There were very few pupils.
(d) He tried to speak their dialect.
(e) He was in a new school.

(f) There were only eight boys.

Festival

Read this passage and then answer the questions at the end.

George was happy indeed. His boyhood ambition to play his cornet in the national championships would be fulfilled the following day. He had come to Larninch, the county town, to take part in this great annual event.

His bandmaster, Sandy McTavish, was so determined to win that he ordered all bandsmen to attend for a last rehearsal early in the morning. After a six o'clock call and a light breakfast, they went to Lewisvin Park. Here a team of officials was already checking the safety of the seats and marking fresh lines where overnight rain had washed away the previous day's work.

Although the morning was pleasant and everyone was looking forward to the afternoon, Sandy was irritable. He was sure something would go wrong as it was Friday the 13th. Surprisingly he conceded that the practice was going "quite well". He would never give high praise lest any of them should become over-confident.

By 1.30 spectators had turned up in their thousands, all looking so relaxed and gay as they waited for the first band to appear. But George now felt butterflies in his stomach. It was the thought of performing in front of so big a crowd.

The bands which had been drawn first, second and third were called in turn. Each one seemed so much better than any he had ever heard. Could his really be a winner? Time would soon tell. Already the announcement was being made. How proud George must have felt as they marched on to the cheers of the happy throng.

Match the effect *in column 1 with the correct* cause *in column 2.*

For example, "1. George was happy because (f) he was to play in the championship," so we could write 1 (f). Do the others in the same way.

1. George was happy.	(a) He wanted to win.
2. New lines were being marked.	(b) The number of people worried him.
3. Sandy McTavish was edgy.	(c) They might become too sure they would win.
4. He did not praise his band.	(d) It was Friday 13th
5. He had an early practice.	(e) Other bands played so well.
6. George was nervous.	(f) He was to play in the championships.
7. George doubted if they would win.	(g) Rain had washed the marks away.

6. Do it this way
Following instructions

RIGHT ORDER

In a previous section we considered reading for detail. Perhaps you need to study details most carefully of all when you are going to follow instructions.

In and out of school you read a great many instructions. If you do not study them carefully, your work will not be accurate.

The order is very important in instructions.

First of all let's check to see if you can recognise the order in which things happen. Read the following passage.

George hurried home and shut himself in his room. Who would be a goalkeeper? Tomorrow all the boys would blame him. "How unjust", he thought.

At the semi-final he had been the hero and he had been carried shoulder-high from the pitch. But today there had been no cheers. As he took up position between the goal posts he remembered Mr Smith's instructions before the game. "Don't throw the ball. Kick it hard up-field." And then in his excitement with two minutes to go he had thrown it to David, but not far enough. The Rovers' forward got it and George's team lost the cup.

The events are told in the following order:

(a) George went home.
(b) He had been the hero.
(c) Mr Smith gave instructions.
(d) The game was lost.
(e) He threw the ball.

But they did not happen in that order.
The first event referred to is the semi-final in which "he had been the hero".
We could write the first answer as "1 (b)".

Complete the others writing in the letter in each case.
1. (b) *2.* (c) *3.* _ *4.* _ *5.* _

Here we were in space, streaking towards the moon. We could once again relax after the stresses and strains of the blast-off.

It seemed so long since we received our last minute instructions before entering the space-craft, and then there was that endless wait until we heard the final seconds of the countdown.

But now that was all in the past. We were on our way and feeling good. Why shouldn't we be in great shape? Our months of hard training, since we volunteered, had not been wasted.

The above events are told in the following order:
(a) in space
(b) instructions
(c) entry into craft
(d) long wait
(e) count down
(f) training
(g) volunteering.

Put them in the order in which they happened. You need only write the letters. The first one is (g); the second one is (f).
1. (g) 2. (f) 3. _ 4. _ 5. _ 6. _ 7. _

Mother and father had saved hard since February to pay for a week's Mediterranean holiday. Although when we turned up at Luton Airport we had to pay an extra £5 for each member of the family, it had been well worth it.

Thursday was the most exciting day of all. It was such fun to snorkel, to water-ski, to swim in the warm sea and to laze in the kindly cooling breeze. It seemed unreal to think that the following morning it would be time to return home.

Away back in January the travel agent had said to us, "You'll enjoy your week in the Mediterranean. It will be the greatest holiday you have ever had." How right he had been.

Tuesday and Wednesday on the small Greek island had been even better than the first three days cruising on the liner.

Some events are mentioned in the following order:
(a) Saving for the holiday
(b) Best day of the holiday
(c) Return home
(d) Travel agent's forecast
(e) Stay in the Greek island
(f) Three days' cruising.

Arrange them in the order in which they happened.
1. (d)   2. _   3. _   4. _   5. _   6. _

Just after midnight on Friday we set off for Glasgow in the new car I had bought the previous day. We drove up the coast road to the outskirts of the town and there the car broke down. As none of us had any money for hotel accommodation we spent the night in the car.

It was by a stroke of good luck that I managed to get home early in the morning. At first light a butcher's van came past. The driver willingly offered us a lift home, but it was not a pleasant journey hanging on to hooks beside large sides of beef.

The events are told in this order:

(a) We set off for Glasgow.

(b) I bought a new car.

(c) The car broke down.

(d) We spent the night in the car.

(e) I arrived home.

(f) We got a lift in a butcher's van.

Put them in the order they happened. Write letters only.
1. _ 2. _ 3. _ 4. _ 5. _ 6.

PICTURE THE STEPS

Now let us look at some of the types of instructions you may come across in and out of school.

In this section you are going to check how carefully you can read and follow instructions.

You will be asked:
1. *to read each set of instructions fairly quickly to get the general idea,*
2. *to read it again slowly, memorising and paying very careful attention to every detail,*
and,
3. *to read it at least once more very carefully before attempting the exercise.*

You may find all the directions difficult to remember.

Practise forming a picture in your mind *of each step as you read.*

Study these instructions (which were taken from a school-book).

> *Read over the following passage quickly.*
> *Read it a second time very carefully.*
> *Read the passage very carefully a third*
> *time before trying the exercise.*

Now turn over and try the first task on the next page without turning back

Which is the correct answer? (See previous page.)

I must read quickly on the (first, second, third) reading.
The second time I must read very (quickly/carefully).
I am asked to read (2, 3, 4) times altogether.

It is important to study instructions with great care.
1. Read them over quickly to get the general idea.
2. Now study them very carefully and note the order.
3. Read them carefully again before you turn to page 77.

Try to form a picture in your mind of each step.

A How to glue surfaces

Clean both surfaces to be glued.

Pierce the nozzle of the tube.

Apply glue to both surfaces. Spread thinly.

Leave 10 minutes to become tacky.

Press together firmly.

Leave for 24 hours.

Try A on page 77 without looking back.

Remember what you must do.
1. Read instructions over quickly.
2. Next read them very carefully and slowly.
3. Read at least once again very carefully.

Try to form a picture in your mind of each step.

B How to plant a bush

Soak roots in water for 24 hours.

Prepare a good hole.

Place the bush in the hole.

Spread the roots out evenly from the centre.

Replace the soil in the hole.

Tread the soil firmly around the bush.

Try B on page 77 without turning back.

Read over quickly. Now study very carefully. Read very carefully at least once more. Build up in your mind a picture of each step.

C How to bake a potato.

 1. Switch on oven.
 2. Scrub potato.
 3. Dry potato on kitchen paper.
 4. Prick potato all over with fork.
 5. Sprinkle potato with salt.
 6. When oven is hot enough, put potato on baking tray.
 7. Put tray with potato on it in oven.
 8. Bake until soft.
 9. Turn oven off.
10. Remove potato from oven.
11. Serve potato with butter or margarine, salt and pepper.

Try C on page 77 without looking back.

D Edward's Evening

Edward intended to watch TV all evening but his mother said, "No. You may watch *Dr Who* now, but then you must do your homework for Monday. Your room has to be tidied up. After that you'll take the magazines to Aunt May, and then, and only then, may you watch TV again."

Try D on page 77.

---

1. *Read these instructions quickly.*
2. *Study them very carefully.*
3. *Read them very carefully at least once more before you try E.*
4. *Build up in your mind a picture of each step.*

E Find Your Way

Get off the bus at the stop in Broad Street

Cross the street at the zebra crossing

and then turn to your right

Walk to the first pillar box

Our house is the fourth past it.

Try E on page 77

F Instructions for Jim

Jim's mother told him to go to the shops. First of all he was to go to the butcher **BUTCHER** for a pound of sausages, next to the baker **BAKER** in the same street for 12 rolls, and then across the road to the dairy **DAIRY** for two cartons of milk. On the way home he was to pay Mr Smith **PAPERS** for the week's papers.

Try F on page 77.

DIRECTIONS

Imagine you have lost your way in a town.
You ask how to get to the railway station.

A policeman says, "Continue along High Street till you come to the corner at Forth Street. Turn left into Forth Street. Walk to the traffic lights. Turn right and walk to the railway station which you will see on your right-hand side."

You may find all the directions difficult to remember. *Try building up a picture in your mind.*

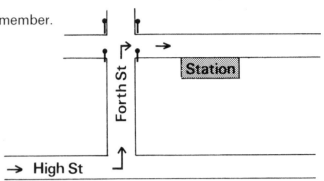

Continue along High Street till you come
to the corner at Forth Street.
Turn left into Forth Street.
Walk to the traffic lights.
Turn right.
Walk to the railway station which
you will see on your right-hand side.

A stranger outside the Bus Station asks you the way to Alpine Grove. All the instructions you would need to give him are set out below, but they are in the wrong order. *Put them in the right order.*

Write letters only 1. _ 2. _ 3. _ 4. _ 5. _.

(a) Turn left into Hope Street.
(b) Walk along Main Street until you come to the Church.
(c) Walk up Hope Street.
(d) Walk along Victoria Street until you come to Alpine Grove on your left.
(e) At the Police Station turn right into Victoria Street.

Write out five instructions you would give to a traveller at the Railway Station who wishes to go to the Grand Hotel.

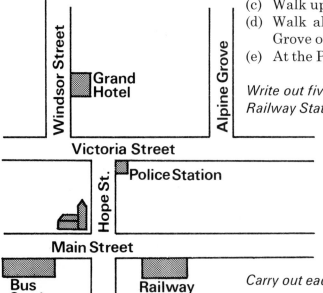

Carry out each of the following instructions carefully.

1. Take a square of paper (side not less than 12 cms).
2. Fold it in half to form a rectangle.
3. Fold it in half again to form a square.
4. Fold the square into a triangle. (You do this by placing one corner on the opposite corner so that the edges previously folded go together.)
5. Press down firmly all three sides of the triangle.
6. Open out the paper and place flat on your desk.
7. Mark the centre with your pencil.
   You have 8 creases coming out from the centre.
8. Turn the paper so that one corner points away from you. Mark this corner N.
9. Work round in a clockwise direction and mark the end of the remaining creases NE, E, SE, S, SW, W, and NW, in that order.
10. Draw lines along the creases but not through the letters you have written.

If you carried out the instructions carefully, you should end up with a diagram of the 8 point compass like the one shown here.

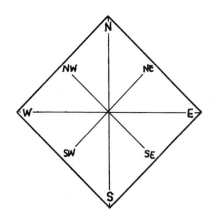

A *How to Glue Surfaces*

Can you fill in the missing instructions without referring back?

?
Pierce the nozzle of the tube.
Apply glue to both surfaces. Spread thinly.
Leave 10 minutes to become tacky.
?
Leave for 24 hours.

B *How to Plant a Bush*

The instructions (A B C D E F) are written in the wrong order.
Can you put them in the correct order?
1. B *2.* _ *3.* _ *4.* F *5.* _ *6.* _.

A Place the bush in the hole.
B Soak the roots for 24 hours.
C Prepare a good hole.
D Tread the soil firmly around the bush.
E Replace the soil in the hole.
F Spread the roots out evenly from
   the centre.

C *How to bake a potato*

What are the missing instructions?

1. Switch on oven.
2. –
3. Dry potato on kitchen paper.
4. –
5. –
6. When oven is hot enough, put potato
   on baking tray.
7. –
8. –
9. Turn oven off.
10. –
11. Serve potato with butter or margarine,
    salt and pepper.

D *Edward's Evening*

What are the missing instructions?

Five things his mother says he will do.
1. Watch *Dr Who*.
2. –
3. –
4. –
5. Watch TV

E *Find Your Way*

What are the missing words?

1. Dismount from the bus.
2. – at the zebra crossing.
3. Turn – .
4. Walk past the pillar box.
5. Our house is the – one past
   the pillar box.

F *Instructions for Jim*

What are the missing words?

1. Go to the butcher for
2. Go to the _ for 12 rolls.
3. Go to the dairy for   –
4. Go to Mr Smith's to pay   –

FLOW CHART

How to bath a dog

1.

2.

3.

4.

5.

6.

7.

8.

How to bath the dog

Opposite there are eight pictures in the correct order. The pictures demonstrate the correct way to bath the dog.
Below are eight instructions.
(a) Get dog;   (b) Wash dog;   (c) Empty bath;   (d) Get bath, towel, soap and water;   (e) Heat water;   (f) Dry dog; (g) Fill bath;   (h) Put dog in bath.

1. *Match an instruction to each picture. Write the answers in your book.*
   The instruction for picture 1 is (d) so we could write the answer as 1d.
2. *In your own book copy the flow chart on this page.*

   Number the spaces 1 to 8.

   In each space write an instruction without looking at the book.

   Try to get all eight in the correct order.

   Only when you have finished, open at this page again to check.

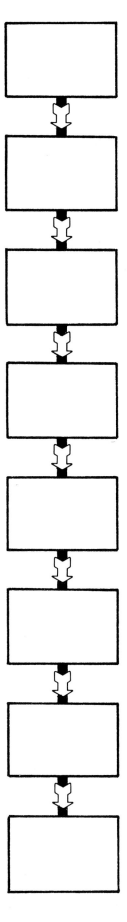

TO FIND A PLACE ON A MAP

1. Refer to the atlas index (*London 17 D1*).
2. Find the name of the place (*London*).
3. After the name there will be a figure (*17*). This tells you the page on which to find the map.
4. After the page number you will find a letter which refers to an area on the map. The letter will be found at the top and the bottom of the map. (London lies in area *D*.)
5. After the letter there will be a number which refers to an area on the map. The numbers are marked down the right and left hand edges. (London lies in area *1* of area *D*.)

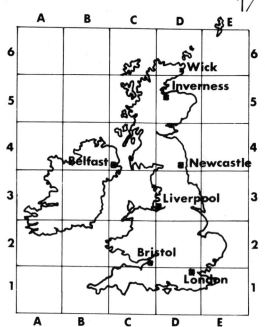

1. London 17 D1.

British Isles

Make up index information for all places named on the map above. You are making up instructions for a person trying to locate those places on a map. (Eg London 17 D1.)

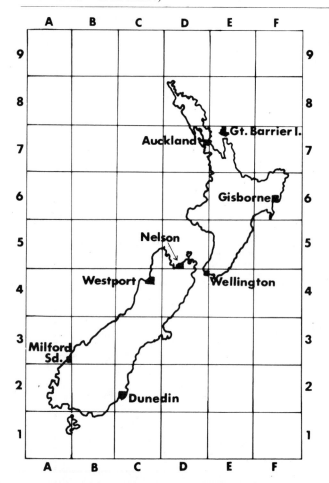

39

Make up index information for the places named on the map of New Zealand.

1. Auckland   39 D7

New Zealand